YOUR GOLF BAG PRO:

Nick Weslock's Little Black Book of Key Golf Secrets

ILLUSTRATIONS:
Neil Harris

Hurtig Publishers
Edmonton

Hurtig Publishers Ltd.
10560 – 105 Street
Edmonton, Alberta
Canada T5H 2W7

Canadian Cataloguing in Publication Data

Weslock, Nick.
  Your golf bag pro

Includes index.
ISBN 0-88830-277-0

1. Golf—Handbooks, manuals, etc.   I. Title.
GV965.W47 1985   796.352′02′02   C85-091131-1

Printed and bound in Canada

Contents

Introduction

A few years ago I was golfing at the Paradise Island course in the Bahamas. As I stood beside the first green, one of my playing companions readied himself to play a chip shot from 25 yards away. I was out of range, or so I thought, but then his ball came tearing through the air right at my head. The ball flew at least 50 yards over the green.

Naturally, I was upset, though thankful the ball had missed me. But I wondered. How could this fellow hit a simple chip shot with so little idea of how hard to hit it? I asked him what he was trying to do. He didn't know.

Since I wanted to protect myself for the rest of the round and figured the man couldn't have enjoyed hitting shots like that, I gave him a tip Gary Player had once given me. "Just feel the force," I told him. By that I meant that he should simply imagine how hard he would have to throw the ball underhand to send it 25 yards, including the roll of the ball after it hit the ground. "Then just hit the ball with the same force."

The tip worked. I was safe for the rest of the game and my companion played what he called the best round of his life, so much did his short game improve. That didn't surprise me. Tips such as this one had helped me many times during a round of golf. All I had to do was dip into one of my little black books that I carried in my golf bag; there I could pick a tip from a collection I had amassed after observing, talking with, and playing with top professionals and amateurs during my golfing life.

This book is a reference guide for golfers. It is meant to be used on and off the course. It contains tips and ideas that have helped me and that can help you. Ever since I was a youngster in Windsor, Ontario, and was fortunate enough to come under the scrutiny of Al Watrous, the head pro at the Oakland Hills Country Club in Birmingham, Michigan, I have paid close attention to what the pros have had to say. Whenever I played with a Gary Player or Tommy Bolt I would ask him what he saw in my game that could be improved. At home I jotted down these thoughts in what became my series of black books.

Not only did I question the top golfers with whom I played, but I also made a point of observing them closely. When I noticed something useful, I put it down. What we have here, then, is a collection of ideas on golf, some gathered through my conversations with players, others through my observations.

Over the years these ideas have helped me and my amateur friends. On occasion they have also helped touring professionals. You might think they don't need help, but the fact is that even they lose their good form from time to time. During the 1974 Canadian Open at Mississauga near Toronto, I was approached by 1973 Masters winner Tommy Aaron. He needed help, since he had been losing distance and was fading the ball. I asked him to set up to the ball. From behind him, I could see that he had allowed his right forearm to creep out so that he had it positioned higher than his left. This effectively weakened his left arm, and tilted his shoulders so that he was aligned left of his target. He couldn't help but cut across the ball from that position, thereby losing distance and slicing his ball to the right of his target. I suggested he pull his right forearm back underneath his left, and that corrected his problem immediately.

That was a tip that worked, and that's what this book includes: tips that work. The only worthwhile tip is one that has a positive effect. These tips have proven themselves. If not for the material here I wouldn't have succeeded in salvaging so many rounds in which I was headed for a high score. The tips are simple, and they are quick. I start with a section on the fundamentals that I consider to be basic to good golf; ingrain these fundamentals into your game. Then, if you are having trouble in a specific area, like chipping, for example, look it up in the appropriate section. There you will find the help you need.

The book, then, consists of keys,

tips, and hints on every part of your game. I do want to make one important point clear. I have not so much put together a theory of the golf swing, but a selection of ideas, many of which will be effective for you just when you need them. You may find some tips contradict others; that won't happen often, but when it does, it's as it should be. Golf, after all, is an individual game, and what works for one person may not work for another.

In general, two things can hurt your game: either the mechanics of your swing break down, and/or you are not thinking properly. These act together, of course, the one influencing the other, and this book takes both into account. The opening section on fundamentals emphasizes mechanics. The section that follows it includes tips for specific shots, but it also incorporates a good deal of philosophy on playing the game. Golf is a game of precision in the swing and in thinking; by referring to both sections of the book you will cover the essential ingredients of the game.

It's important to realize and

accept that golf *is* a precision game. Your swing might very well feel different from one day to the next. That's fine; you are not a machine and you cannot hit perfect shots every time. But you *can* hit *better* shots; you *can* salvage a round that begins badly and experience one of golf's greatest pleasures: turning your game around quickly. This book will perk you up when things are looking grim; it will give you hope. Carry it in your golf bag and don't hesitate to refer to it when you have difficulties.

During my career as an amateur golfer I have won the Canadian Amateur four times and the Ontario Amateur eight times. I was low amateur in the Canadian Open sixteen times, and have represented Canada many times on international teams. I do not cite these statistics to impress you. What I *would* like to point out is that I still have needed plenty of help along the way. I started with Al Watrous fifty years ago, and I'm still learning. In fact I'm certain the learning process will never stop. It

was with the hope of transmitting
to you some of what I *have* learned
that I decided to put the best of all
my black books together in this
easy-to-use form.

Because I am an amateur golfer,
I am not allowed to accept money
from the writing or sale of this book.
If I did, I would have to forfeit my
amateur status. I didn't want to do
that as a player and certainly don't
wish to do so as a writer. However,
the money will go to a very worthy
cause. Revenue from this book will
be distributed according to a plan
Mel Hurtig of Hurtig Publishers and
I have agreed upon. It will enable
me to give back to golf some of
what I have enjoyed over the years.

All royalties from the sales of this
book will be shared on an equal
basis between the Junior Develop-
ment Fund of the Ontario Golf
Association and the scholarship
program of the Canadian Golf
Foundation, an arm of the Royal
Canadian Golf Association. The
proceeds, then, will aid amateur
golf in Canada. I consider this small
payment for the great pleasure I
have had playing golf around the
world and meeting fine people

wherever I went. Golf has been the greatest game of all for me, and I am happy to be able to contribute in this way to the sport in Canada.

It's also very satisfying to think that this book will help many men and women improve their game. So, for all those golfers who know they *can* improve, here are my thoughts on just how to go about it.

Nick Weslock

Fundamentals

A/The grip: Take a club in your left hand. The butt or top end of the shaft should be placed under the inside of the heel pad on your left hand (the pad opposite your little finger). Two knuckles on the left hand should be visible to you at address. Apply the right hand square to the target line, with the *palms of your hands opposing each other*. The little finger of the right hand will overlap the forefinger of your left hand, fitting just between your forefinger and middle finger.

Most of the pressure in your grip should come from the *last three fingers of your left hand*. At the top of your swing you should be able to maintain a firm grasp of the club with just these three fingers and the club against the heel pad. Right-hand pressure should be light and comfortable with *little or no pressure from the thumb and forefinger*. This grip will promote your hands working as a unit throughout the swing. Our present-day tour players favour a hand position where the Vs formed by the thumb and forefinger of both hands point more to the right eye rather than to the right shoulder as in the past.

B/Stance and ball position: Your stance should be shoulder width for your long game, with the ball placed on the target line 2 inches to the right of your left heel. As the clubs get shorter, *the ball stays in the same relationship* to your left heel. You simply narrow your stance by bringing your right foot toward your left.

C/Posture: Stand upright, then relax into the natural golfing position as you set the club down. Your knees will be slightly bent; the general attitude will be that of a person sitting on a tall bar stool.

D/Alignment to the target: Stand 6 to 8 feet behind the ball. Select a spot or divot 3 to 6 inches in front of your ball along the line to your target. Approach the ball and set the club behind it, feet together, with your clubhead at a right angle

Fig. 1 The Grip.
The predominant pressure should be with the last three fingers of your left hand. Exert firm pressure with the little finger of your right hand to ensure unity.

Light pressure should also be exerted with the rest of the right hand. Pressure from the thumb and forefinger should be especially light.

The Vs should point to your chin and no further than your right eye. You should see two knuckles of the left hand, and your right palm should be square to the line.

to your target. Now your feet, knees, hips, and shoulders should be square to the target. Widen the stance so that it's appropriate to your shot. Repeat this procedure for every shot.

E/Weight distribution at address: Your weight should be predominantly towards your heels, and on the balls of the feet rather than towards your toes. If you turn your toes up just a bit you will more easily achieve the desired weight distribution which promotes the balance so necessary to an efficient swing.

F/Shoulder and arm positions at address: *Tilt your left shoulder up* so that the right forearm is lower than the left forearm. This promotes a low takeaway and causes the club to go straight back instead of outside the line. This is very important and a *major key* to a good swing.

G/Neck area tension: I include this because it causes golfers so many problems. There is no need to live with this very common tension. You want to feel *loose and free* while setting up a shot. If your neck is stiff and pulled into your shoulders, you will create an imbalance. The tension in the neck and *resultant tightness across your shoulders* is likely to inhibit a free swing. To stay relaxed, simply drop your shoulders so that they are hanging, all the while keeping your chin up. This is crucial both in the regular swing and when putting – actually, with every club in the bag!

H/Visualizing the flight path:

While in a relaxed and ready position at address, visualize the desired flight path of the ball to your target. Focus *above* the target to encourage a free swing *through* the ball rather than a swing *at* it; this visualization is an essential component of every good golfer's preparation. It acts as a trigger for your swing.

I/Takeaway: Point your chin at the ball during address and through the swing, thereby ensuring that your left shoulder will have *room to move under your chin on the*

Fig. 2   Weight Distribution and Posture at Address.
Stand tall. Flex your knees slightly as if you were about to sit on a high stool.

Your weight should be predominantly on the heels and balls of your feet; turning your toes up inside your shoes achieves this. Putting your weight on your toes, on the other hand, destroys your balance.

*Fig. 3   Shoulder and Forearm
Positions at Address.
Your shoulder to the clubhead
should form a single line, and the
shoulders and hips should be
square to the target line.*

*The right foot is square, the left foot
turned about 40° towards the hole.
The left shoulder should be tilted
up, with the right forearm always
below the left.*

*The shoulders and neck area
should feel loose, so that any
tension is eliminated.*

*Fig. 4 Starting the Backswing.
The position of the ball on the target
line is always about 2 inches to the
right of the left heel.*

*Keep your head steady; it's the
point of the compass. Relax your
arms and stretch them just before
the takeaway. Brush the grass
behind the ball going back, 10 to 14
inches with woods, and 6 to 8
inches with long and middle irons.
Point the left knee at the ball and
keep the right knee locked in
position while rotating the hips.*

*Keep your chin up and your left
shoulder under the chin for the full
turn.*

way back. To help create a smooth tempo, sole the blade of your club lightly. This also helps you maintain the posture you start with. Couple this with *brushing the grass* with the sole of your club for the first 6 to 8 inches of your takeaway. Your hands will consequently work as a unit, moving in a wide arc on the takeaway. (If you pick up the club, a very common fault, the arc becomes smaller, your backswing gets faster, and you lose power and accuracy.) Turn your head slightly to the right for a bigger shoulder turn and press the hands forward fractionally just before swinging to break down tension which might have built up at address.

J/Knee action and hip turn: As you begin your swing, point your left knee towards the back of the ball to influence the turning of your right hip. At the top of your swing the left knee will be pointing behind the ball as you have swung into a fully coiled position. You can also get into the right position at the top by turning your right pocket away from the ball on your backswing.

The right hip turn is an important key, like pulling back on a bow. It creates potential energy which will be released as you come through the ball and it *keeps the swing path on the inside-to-out coming through*.

K/Position at the top: At this point the back of your left wrist should be flat, *not cupped*. This encourages the proper position of your right elbow, pointing down at the ground. The back of your left wrist should be parallel to the clubface, with the shaft pointing down the line towards your target. The leading edge of the clubface should be pointing to a 4:30 o'clock position. At the top of the backswing, the back of the left hand and forearm form a straight line.

L/Downswing: The first move down is a transfer of your weight to your left foot and left side. This takes place *before* you start the club down. Going through, you should feel as if you are hitting under the ball and up, focussing above your target and keeping

Fig. 5   Position of the Left Wrist at the Top of the Backswing.
For all shots, from the driver through to the pitching wedge, your left wrist must be parallel with the left forearm, *and not cupped.*
Among other things, this prevents a flying right elbow.

Fig. 6   The Downswing, and Through Impact.
The first move on the downswing is to transfer your weight to the left leg.

Make a concerted effort to keep your head steady. There shouldn't be any movement upwards, downwards, or laterally.

The right knee drives down the line, influencing the turning of the right hip. Focus on the back of the ball, not the top of the ball. The face of the club continues through impact square to your line.

*Fig. 7   Position at the Finish.
A full pivot through to the finish,
with the shaft hitting your back,
assures a complete swing and
avoids deceleration during the
swing.*

the clubface square to the target through impact.

M/The finish: Never lose sight of the fact that you want to *finish with the shaft behind your back*. You are now standing at your full height, facing the target, with all your weight on your left foot. Your weight has been carried there by the acceleration of the clubhead through the ball. You should finish in balance, poised, and looking down the line. Any tendency to cut off your full follow-through usually results in an off-line shot, deceleration, and coming up short of your target.

N/And, an overall key: Maintain a *steady* head position during the swing. This cannot be overemphasized. It is a factor on which everything else depends. Ignore this vital key and you will never have a consistent swing.

On the Way to the Golf Course

1

Be gung-ho. Look forward to playing. Plan your day so that you can get to the course in plenty of time. Imagine yourself hitting good shots. Imagine a player whose swing you like, whose timing and tempo you would like to emulate.

2

Prepare your mind for the challenge of a round of golf. Think of achieving your goal, whether it's attacking par or playing even bogey golf.

3

Having set your goal, accept that. You know your capabilities. Your potential is limited only by the soundness of your swing and your ability to manage your game. Both can be worked on. Think of how you play when your swing is smooth and your concentration is at a peak. That is your upper limit. Strive for it.

4

Challenge yourself, but not so much that you will feel strained or ill-at-ease. If you're an 18 handicap and your course rating is 71, set yourself a target score of 86. Try to plan your way around the course so that you won't score more than a bogey on any hole.

5

Keep in mind that a good performer – and golfers are performers – has these characteristics: intelligence, composure, a feeling of involvement, desire, stamina and conditioning, a solid grasp of technique and the fundamentals, confidence, a humility that keeps him or her from becoming complacent, and the ability to practise with a purpose and stick to it, plus a "never-say die" attitude.

General Practice

6

Develop timing and rhythm. Isolate the parts of your swing that need work. Concentrate on a specific aspect that needs attention. Ignore results when first working on changes. Pay attention to the scoring parts of golf: the pitching wedge, sand wedge, greenside play, and putting.

7

Visit pro tournaments in your area. Observe what the top players have in common. Examine their routine with each shot. Notice how the players take the club back, how their hips turn, the position of their hands and wrists at the top, how they start down to the ball, and how they orbit through to the finish with the club behind the back. Pay particular attention to the pros' timing, shoulder turns, and leg drives. Watch also how the pros accelerate through the ball after a *smooth, slow backswing.*

8

Begin your practice sessions with a pitching wedge or sand iron. Then go through the middle irons, long irons, and on to the fairway woods and driver.

9

Visualize the shots you are practising. Simulate shots you will face during the round.

10 █████████████████

Focus on a tangible object in the distance, be it a tree, practice flag, or bunker. Be target-oriented. Shape your shot to the picture you have visualized. Involve yourself in the ball's flight.

11 █████████████████

Keep your practice sessions interesting. Try different shots. Play finesse shots over bunkers. Hit sand shots from various positions and lies. Hit fades, draws, punch shots, and high trajectory and low trajectory shots. Stay interested. Stay stimulated. Stay motivated.

12 █████████████████

On the putting green, hit your first putts from about 5 feet from the hole. Put some balls in a semi-circle and stroke them into the hole, paying attention to fundamentals. Move back to 10 feet, 20 feet, 30 feet, and hit a few from even longer range. Try downhill, uphill, and sidehill putts.

13

Practise on the course only when it's quiet. Go out in the evening with a couple of balls and play one against the other for three or four holes. Or play "worst ball," where you hit two balls and go to the one in the worst position, carrying on from there with the two balls. This builds concentration. You won't want to hit into the rough after you've hit one on the green.

Pre-Game Warm-Up

14

Avoid getting too swing-conscious. Remember what Lee Trevino said:

on the course you've got to dance with the girl you brought to the ballroom. The same is true on the practice green before you play. You're not trying to find a new stroke, but simply getting the feel of the greens that day.

15

If your course has a practice range, hit some shots to loosen up. Begin with the shorter irons and work your way through the bag, hitting just a few shots with each club. Don't spend more than 20 minutes or so practising. You are there to loosen up. Swing fully and comfortably with a good, smooth tempo.

16

To gauge the speed of the greens while chipping and putting, I rely on a tip I received from Gary Player after practice rounds with him in the 1957 Masters. He suggested I "*feel the force*," that is, imagine how hard I would have to roll the ball underhand to get it to the hole. This has been a lifesaver for me many times. It's useful on the putting green, for chip shots, and especially worthwhile in sand traps.

To learn how to "feel the force," stand on the apron of the green and toss a ball underhand to the hole. Feel the force you had to use to toss it for the distance, and then hit a shot with the same force. Alternate throwing and hitting.

17

While practising your chipping and putting, be quiet and stable over the ball. You're looking for a "zone of calmness." You have gone from the full swing on the range to the quieter play around the practice green. Allow yourself to get into the new beat. By the time you leave the putting green you will want to have something you can count on, what the British golf teacher Percy

Boomer called a "remembered feel." Your goal is to build in the right feel through the right methods.

18

Prior to teeing off, hit about a dozen chip shots and putts. The idea is to ingrain a feel for the greens in your mind. You're priming your senses for action. You're continuing to program yourself for play on the course by previewing the shots.

19

During your warm-up, allow yourself to get just a bit more excited as your time to play draws closer. You don't want that first tee feeling to be a surprise. There isn't a golfer in the world who doesn't feel a bit of a surge of adrenalin on the first tee. Know that you'll feel it. During your last practice swings, pretend that you're already there. That's good preparation for the walk to the first tee, which many golfers say is the longest walk in golf. With the correct preparation, it can be an invigorating stroll rather than a fearful hike.

The First Tee

20

The first tee is where you learn that no matter how much in control you might be, you are still vulnerable and fragile. No matter how self-contained you might have become in your well-thought-out warm-up, and no matter how nicely stimulated you might have become in your last few practice shots, you may still find yourself in a bit of a frenzy at the tee. Remember that *every golfer feels something of the same concern*.

21 ████████████████

Golfers who play to their potential from the first tee on have learned to deal with their heightened state of emotion. Almost any golfer can learn to do this. The secret lies in learning how to relax at will and thereby bringing yourself back from too much excitement to a calmer, yet stimulated state.

22 ████████████████

While on the first tee, do this simple exercise for relaxation. Put your right hand in front of the club shaft at one end with your palm facing forward. (The shaft will be lying across the back of your right hand.) Hook your right thumb over the shaft and put the club behind your back. Do the same thing with your left hand at the other end of the club. Turn your shoulders to and fro about a dozen times.

Fig. 8 First Tee Warm-up and Relaxing Exercise.
For the upper shoulders and neck area, *place the club behind your back as illustrated, with the thumbs hooked over the shaft and the palms facing forward. Rotate to the left and right, back and forth.*

For your lower back, place the club shaft across the small of your back. Hook the inside of your elbows around the shaft and rotate your body back and forth.

23 ████████████████

Once over the ball, let your shoulders hang. Keep the tension out of the neck. That's where trouble starts. Keep the neck loose and the shoulders hanging. You'll get that wonderful feeling of freedom: freedom of motion, freedom of arm stretch, freedom of turn. You'll begin to realize that the golf swing is meant to be enjoyed. That's the great thing about the swing: it's physically relaxing. So be sure not to let tension interfere with your enjoyment of golf.

During the Round
████████████████

24 ████████████████

Play reasonably, not rashly. Resist the temptation to recover in one stroke shots already dropped during the round. Play safely if you find yourself in a difficult situation.

25

Play the golf course as if it were a chess-board, as far as your abilities allow you to do so. Whatever level you play, beginner or grand master, you can plan and follow a game plan. Your shots are the moves you make to manoeuvre your way around the course. They are your decisions. Make them as sensible decisions as you can, but accept that you will certainly make errors.

26

Think and imagine where you are capable of placing the ball if you swing smoothly and within yourself. Motivate yourself. Think of how pleasant it is going to be out on the course, either with your friends or with new players, trying to meet the 18-hole challenge. Relish the challenge. Your motivation will increase accordingly. You will reduce your anxiety as you become more involved. This comes from playing *your* game. You are a unique golfer with your own abilities, characteristic responses, and inclinations.

27

While your company on the course is likely to be pleasant, remember that golf is an individual game. You are playing on and against the course, an ever-present challenge. Be cordial to your playing companions, but do not get involved in their games. Converse with them, but maintain concentration on your own game once you get to your ball.

28

I once asked Arnold Palmer how he motivated himself when he played with amateurs. He said he had but one opponent, "old man par." Every time Arnie steps up to the ball, it's just him, the ball, the course, and his plan. When he's ready to play, he completely eliminates from his mind the fact that other golfers are present.

29

Accept the fact that some days you have it and others you don't. Play within yourself and with what you have that day. You are a human being, not a machine. And, sometimes, take a rest: don't get over-golfed. (Actually, one of those rest days is a good time to pull this book out of your bag!)

The Driver

30

The driver is undoubtedly the most difficult club to control because the intent is to apply force for maximum distance. This tends to bring out our desire to hit the ball hard. Instead, plant these thoughts in your mind: *effortless power*, not powerful effort; *centrifugal force*, not brute force; *let the clubhead do the work*; *eliminate the hit impulse*; and *swing the club*.

31

Aim. Pick your target. Keep in mind that your objective is to move the ball from point A to point B. You want to hit the ball *as straight as possible* and let the distance take care of itself. *Keep the ball in play.*

32

Strategy is all-important when you have the driver in your hands. Remember, it's easier to play your ball from the fairway than from the rough, traps, or trees. You obviously want to feel satisfied with your drive and there's no better way than to knock your ball down the fairway. You feel smart, you feel sharp, you feel in control. *Plan your drive to give it the best chance of landing on the fairway.*

Select a spot on the tee that plays away from trouble and always be target-conscious.

33

Get comfortable on the tee by moving around before it's time to tee off. Find a level area, one that gives you a view of the hole with which you feel satisfied.

34

The big key with the driver is to *take the club back low to the ground*, brushing the surface of the grass for the first 12 to 14 inches back. This will promote a wide arc which will help create centrifugal force.

35

Orbit to the finish, letting yourself go to a *full finish* position, in balance, and with the shaft behind your back.

Fairway Woods

36

Once we move away from the tee towards the green, we tend to get too target-oriented, that is, excessively focussed on placing our ball just so. In our efforts to get where we want to, we tend to try to guide the ball. Remember, just *swing towards your target*. Your objective is to place the ball for your next shot.

37

The loft of the fairway woods is designed to get the ball airborne and give you maximum distance in flight. Let the loft control the trajectory and distance. Learn how far you hit your shots with a smooth swing and if you are tempted to smash the ball, step away. *Take it easy. Swing the club.*

38

There is no need to overswing the fairway woods. Play within yourself and you will be in position more frequently and score lower. You'll get nearer the par-fives in two and even reach some. *Focus on tempo.*

Long Irons (1,2,3)

39

These clubs are normally very difficult for the amateur golfer. The mental approach should be to think in terms of *sweeping the ball off the fairway* rather than taking a divot. *Execute the same full swing as you would with the fairway woods or a driver.*

Fig. 9   The Long Irons.
The key thought to keep in mind is
to use the same swing as with your
driver or fairway woods. Sweep
the ball off the fairway. Take no
divot and execute a full swing.

40

Brush the grass on your takeaway. Focus your eyes *under* the ball rather than on its top. This will help you keep your head back and enable you to get the ball up. It's also a good idea to set the edge of the blade under the ball, at address or close to your point of impact, as this promotes a more exacting hit. Many golfers set the blade too far back of the ball rather than right under the ball.

41

Remember to always pick a spot 8 to 10 inches ahead of your ball along the target line. Continue the clubhead along that line before finishing your follow-through.

Middle Irons (4,5,6)

42

With these clubs, club selection becomes increasingly important. We are usually trying to hit the green with these clubs. The key is to pick enough club to let you swing in good tempo. Abandon all idea of hitting the ball harder; instead take one club more. It's impossible to play accurate golf while forcing a shot.

43

Forget about taking a big divot. *Take a bacon-strip sized divot* rather than a pork-chop divot. By concentrating on the longer, thinner bacon-strip divot, you will stay with the shot longer. This longer extension to the hole gives you a better follow-through. It enables you to maintain the wide arc and to hit your shots straighter along the target line.

44

The bacon-strip or shallow divot is achieved by keeping your posture relatively upright and, most importantly, by combing the grass for at least 6 inches on the takeaway to produce a wide arc, rather than breaking the hands too soon, which would result in a deeper descending blow.

45

To further encourage the bacon-strip divot, maintain a *very steady head position throughout the swing*. That will keep you from diving into the shot and hitting it fat.

Short Irons (7,8,9)

46

These are the scoring clubs. Give them their due. Use them not only on the course but frequently in your practice sessions. It's a great feeling to stick a shot in there close to the hole. It's also a great feeling to save par from the fairway or rough. Every golfer makes mistakes on the way to the green. But you can save many shots with the short irons setting up one-putt greens.

47

Accuracy is everything with these clubs. You take care of the accuracy to a large degree by ensuring that you *keep your shoulders square*. But, because you also want to get your legs and particularly your right knee moving towards the target, *open your hips* at address. Keep 75 per cent of your weight on your left side at address; this will help prevent your making a big turn going back, which isn't required.

48

Because the short irons are quite upright in lie, and shorter in length, *your hands will be closer to your body* and you will bend a bit more from the waist. *Your head and eyes will be just about over the ball*, further promoting an upright, straight-back, and straight-through clubhead path.

49

It's vital that you *keep your head steady* on every shot, but it's especially important as you get nearer the hole. Any error is accentuated. If you're using a driver and you're 30 feet off-line, you're likely still on the fairway. If you're using a short iron, and you're off by that much, often you'll be in a green-side bunker, or worse.

50

Strategy, then, is very important. Don't get fancy. If the pin is cut close to a trap, play away from the hole. After all, being 20 feet left of the hole is better than being buried in a bunker. Play the percentage shot.

51

As the irons get shorter, your hands will feel more active, as they should. There is a sensation of a right-hand hit. This is always against the left hand, which resists the right hand turning the face over or closing it. You should *feel that the ball is climbing the clubface*; don't let your left wrist turn over when the club hits the ball.

52

A good way to drive the right knee to the target is to come off the right heel and up onto the toes of the right foot as you swing through the ball. This is a thrusting, shifting-of-weight motion. It's *not* a sliding of the right or left foot.

Pitching Wedge

53

The construction of this club is important. A proper pitching wedge should have a convex rolled sole, so that the leading edge will not snag the grass as you slide the club under the ball; that is, the leading edge and the sole should be rounded, to help you take a shallower divot. A sharper leading edge may cause you to stick the club in the ground, creating a deeper divot and preventing the sort of crisp, pinching action that is desirable for the pitching wedge.

54

Just before takeaway, firm up, *stretching your arms from shoulders to wrists*. Your eyes should be *directly over the ball*. The club is upright, so with your eyes over the ball, you will more easily bring the club straight back and straight through. *Comb the grass for 6 to 8 inches going back and going through*, allowing your shoulders to control the stroke.

55

The shot with a pitching wedge is a snappy shot. So keep accelerating through the impact, your head steady, left side leading, and right knee driving to the hole. This is predominantly a right-hand hit.

Fig. 10   Wedge Shot with Maximum Bite.

A dual or rolled-bottom wedge is most effective to produce backspin and bite.

The wrists must be passive; the stroke is produced by the shoulders and arms.

On the takeaway, stretch your arms from your armpits to your hands. The sole of the club should brush the turf for 6 to 8 inches back of and through the ball.

The face of the club must not turn over. You should feel that the ball is climbing the face.

Finally, drive the right knee toward the target.

Around the Green, Within 30 Yards

56

The most important thing is to *feel the force.*(See #16.)

57

Consider a typical shot: your ball is on the fairway and the pin is 25 feet from the front edge of the green. You are about 20 feet from the edge. The green is firm and fast.

Place your feet open to the target with 70 per cent of your weight on your left side. Assume a narrow stance, since you will need very little, if any, turnaway from the ball. Place the ball about 2 inches inside your right foot, with your shoulders square to the target line. Grip the club short, eyes directly over the ball. This is a hands and arms shot, a "feel" shot. Pick the club up

sharply on the backswing,
allowing a descending blow that
will produce maximum backspin.

58

Another shot: assume the ball is
lying in 4 inches of rough, with 30
feet of sand between you and the
edge of the green. You are 10 feet
lower than the surface of the green
and the pin is cut 20 to 25 feet from
the edge of the green. In this case,
select your sand wedge and lay it
open. Keep nearly all your weight
on your left side, assume an open
and narrow stance, and sit more
deeply to the ball. Break the wrists
up quickly on the takeaway, and let
the club drop down about 2 to 3
inches behind the ball. Hit with
your right hand, smoothly and
slowly, but completing the swing,
as you would a trap shot. The ball
will come up high and soft with
very little roll after it hits the green.

59

The preceding shot can also be played in another way. Lay the clubface open and take a wider stance to minimize body movement. The backstroke for this "dead lob" shot takes place with the *shoulders only – no wrists*. Keep the arms passive, the head steady, and simply drop the club under the ball. It will pop right up and land very softly.

60

For a soft shot over a greenside trap from the fairway lay open your sand iron or pitching wedge. Rest your right elbow on your right hip keeping it anchored there. This is entirely a wrist-activated stroke. Break up quickly and go through with little arm action. This demands considerable practice but is most effective.

Chipping

61

The more you can duplicate the putting stroke, the better your chances are of chipping near the hole. From 2 to 5 feet off the green select a 4 or 5-iron. Play the ball from a stance that approximates your putting stance. (See tips #81-97.) Also assume a putting grip (reverse overlap, with the index finger of your left hand riding between the little finger and second finger of your right hand). *Use your putting stroke.*

62

As you move away from the green you need to choose a more lofted club for chipping. Your objective is to land the ball on the green and let it run along to the hole as if it were a putt. So select a club with enough loft to get you onto the putting green with minimum ground interference.

Fig. 11 The Dead Lob.
Take a wide stance.

The idea is to slip the club under the ball. No wrist is needed in this shot. Stretch your arms just before the takeaway. Brush the grass on the way back and through, with only your shoulders executing the stroke. Use a sand iron or pitching wedge.

Fig. 12 Chipping Using a Putting Stroke.
On the fairway or on the carpet of the green from 2 to 5 feet from the putting surface, select a 4 or 5-iron and employ your putting grip and putting stance. Stroke through to the hole with the same force you would use with a putter.

Keep the blade low and continue through as you would on your putts. Use the same force as you would if you were rolling the ball underhand to the hole.

Use the same technique on somewhat longer shots with more lofted clubs. Just make sure the shot lands the ball on the green.

63

In heavy rough near the green, close the face of your sand wedge. Break the hands up quickly and sharply and work the right wrist, going through so that the clubface is propelled into a sharp upward finishing arc.

64

From fairly heavy fairway grass only a foot or two off the green, and little green to work with, use a sand iron or pitching wedge. Keep the left arm in close and firm and use a putting stroke, hitting the middle or equator of the ball with the leading edge of the blade.

65

For a high soft lob with the sand wedge, grip the club lightly in the fingers of your right hand. Lay the club open and break your wrists up quickly. Drop the clubface behind the ball softly, using plenty of right wrist.

This shot is useful when your ball is well down in the grass and when you have quite a bit of green to work with.

66

Another way to play a chip from a tight lie near the green, with a good deal of green to work with: Use your shoulders only. Play the ball off your right heel, hands ahead of the ball, and hit a low, running shot. Use a 7 or 8-iron.

Greenside Sand Play

67

Golfers fear the sand because the environment seems intimidating, since it requires a departure from other shots. Here, of course, you don't want to hit the ball first and knock it over the green; you want to hit a cushion of sand. That makes the trap an alien environment for golfers, one in which it's important to feel comfortable by understanding the proper technique.

68

A sand iron must have proper bounce so that it doesn't dig into the sand; you want the leading edge to be rounded and thick, so that it can ride under the ball, picking it up on a cushion of sand. I recommend a D-8 swingweight.

69

Approach the sand trap with a cat-like feeling; stealthy, light of foot. Be quiet, be slow, feel loose. This shot depends on feel and sensitivity. *Emulate the underhand toss technique (see #16) to gauge the force you need to use.*

70

Imagine the ball floating up on a cushion of sand. You're going to provide that cushion by sliding the clubface under the ball and following through. You'll swing almost in slow motion. Feature a light grip and keep the clubface quite open but with your left hand under or in a weak position.

71

The basics: Let your shoulders hang. Grip the club lightly and sit deeper than usual. Pick a grain of sand 2 inches behind the ball and feel the force with which you want to strike it. Open your stance, break up fast with your right hand and take the club back outside the line. Don't quit. Go right through the sand and finish the swing with legs sliding smoothly toward the target.

Fig. 13   The Normal Sand Shot. Weaken the grip slightly with the left hand and open the club face. The right hand completely controls the swing.

The backswing starts with an early wrist break outside the line. Focus on a grain of sand about 2 inches behind the ball; this is where the club should enter the sand. The path of the club creates a slicing action under the ball.

An important key is that the sand iron should be a D-8 swingweight with a bounce sole.

The force used should be that of tossing a ball underhand to the flag.

72

An uphill lie: More resistance to the sand is encountered, so that you have to make a complete follow-through. The ball is played forward, about opposite your left foot. Lay the clubface square to the target and concentrate on hitting about 1 inch behind the ball. The ball will normally come out high and land with very little roll.

73

A downhill lie: Play the ball somewhere between the centre of your stance and more toward your right foot. Stand fairly "open" but set the blade square to the ball. You must break the hands up fast and plan to enter the sand at least 3 inches behind the ball and finish the swing.

74 ███████████████████

A sidehill lie, ball below your feet:
With the left hand slightly under the grip, grip the club near the end to compensate for the slope. Open the clubface slightly, get into a slightly deeper sitting position, and keep the head set throughout the stroke. Break up fast with your hands as with *all* sand shots near the green and try to hit down into the sand about 2 inches behind the ball. Remember a nice, full finish.

75 ███████████████████

A sidehill lie, ball above your feet:
Aim to the right of the flag, with the clubface slightly open. Play the ball inside of your left heel and plan on entering the sand about 1 inch behind the ball with the usual outside-to-in swing path, again completing the swing.

76

The ball below the lip, partially buried or plugged: The main thing is to establish a solid stance. Again, once this is achieved, hold your head position. The face of the club, if it's an uphill lie, must be closed. Now apply a hard blow, entering the sand about 1 inch behind the ball, and just bury the clubhead into the sand with no follow-through.

77

Sand shot, from wet sand: The clubface should be open or laid off, the left hand set under or in a weak position and the right hand in a normal position. This takes the club slightly outside the line. Your stance should be open with the ball 1 inch inside the left heel. The clubhead should enter the sand about 1 inch back of the ball and force should be applied a little harder than usual to a full finish.

78

Sand shot, poached or fried egg lie: The clubface should be hooded or closed. Plan to enter the sand at the back edge of the crater and exert a strong effort to hit down, allowing for a low trajectory and more run than usual. You won't be able to spin the ball because you won't be able to get much club under it. Play the ball further back in your stance with your hands ahead. Break up sharply and feel you are burying the club with the face closed into the sand between the edge of the crater and the ball. There is no need – indeed it's very difficult – to follow through. And pray a little as this is a toughie.

79

Sand shot, deep trap with overhanging lip, with ball below, but a good lie: In this situation, something you will encounter in a "pot bunker," the player requires extraordinary skill. Firstly, the face

*Fig. 14   A Buried or Poached Egg
Lie in a Bunker.
Dig your feet in thoroughly.*

The face of the club should be
square to the hole.

*Your right hand should dominate
the swing. Use a very upright
swing and bury the clubhead into
the sand about 3 inches behind the
ball. No follow-through is necessary.*

of the sand iron must be laid off almost flat. The body, feet, and shoulders must be open and the left hand grip decidedly weak or under the grip. The backswing must be "very upright" with the right hand extremely active both when entering the sand and when exiting it. Full follow-through must be activated to get the ball up fast. If there's a substantial lip to the bunker between you and the hole, you might have to play away from the flag. Fine – at least you'll get out. We all know it's demoralizing to leave a shot in the trap.

80

Long bunker shot near the green: Play the ball more towards your right foot. Use the same technique as from greenside bunkers (See #69, 70 and 71). The only change you need to make is to feel a bit more aggressive when walking into the bunker, according to the length of the shot and the force required.

Putting

██████████████████████████

81 ████████████████████

Most putting errors come from excessive motion. *Keep as stable as possible*. You want very little body or head motion except on long putts, where some motion is acceptable. Only the arms move as you make your stroke. Your eyes should be directly over the ball.

82 ████████████████████

Putting is a very personal aspect of golf. Players tend to find their own methods to achieve the stability that's necessary. Following is a compendium of ideas, some of which you might find helpful at different times when a problem arises in putting.

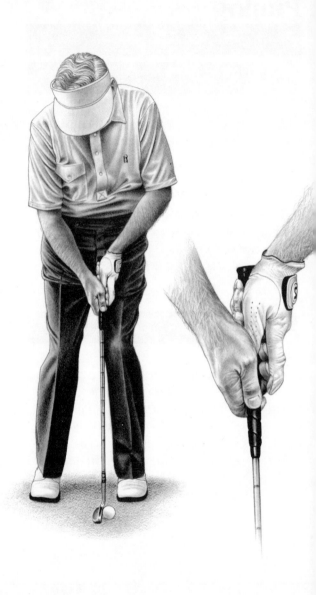

Fig. 15   The Putting Stroke.
Grip the club lightly, using a reverse
overlap grip. The left forefinger
overlaps 1, 2 or 3 fingers of the right
hand. Both thumbs point straight
down the grip so the Vs point
toward your chin.

Stay loose in your neck area and
stand perfectly still with your
weight predominantly on your left
heel, for stability.

Sole the putter blade lightly just
before the takeaway to promote a
smooth stroke. Stroke through the
ball to the hole, not just at the ball.

83

Use a reverse overlap grip. This takes more of the left hand out of the putting stroke. The left hand guides the club; it's the direction hand. The right hand is mainly used to sense acceleration but it also controls accuracy to a certain extent, since the right palm should go directly along the target line.

84

Select a putter whose blade you can feel. It ought to be about a D-1 swingweight and lie fairly upright to encourage you to keep your eyes over the ball. This also keeps the wrists in a bowed position, locked with the forearms. This prevents a "wristy" stroke, which is never consistent, nor will it hold up under pressure.

85

The Vs in your grip point to your chin. Putt without wrist break. *Do not follow the ball to the hole*. Hear it drop, especially on the short ones.

86

The pressure in your right hand should come from your middle finger. Place both thumbs on the top of the grip.

87

Before your stroke, take a long, slow look along the line to the hole and back to the ball. Sole the blade lightly behind the ball. Then stroke the ball. Always repeat the same pattern every time. Swivel your head back and forth when looking over your line – don't raise it.

88

Visualize a good roll; do not dwell on the mechanics.

89

Take the time to look over your putt. When you are ready to putt, step up, take two practice strokes to feel the force, square the blade to your line, take one or two looks (according to your routine), and then stroke the ball. Keep your eyes on the back of the ball until the stroke has been completed.

90

It's best to putt with passive or quiet wrists. But it's not always easy. To keep them quiet, *wring your hands towards each other* just before the stroke. This will minimize any wrist activity.

91

Square the back of the left hand to the target line as well as the palm of the right hand. Your right elbow should just graze your right hip through your stroke. *Do not change the "set" of the arms and/or elbows during the stroke.*

92

On short putts, aim at a spot at the back of the hole.

93

On longer putts pick a spot a foot or two ahead of the ball and on your line; set up square to this spot and stroke through and over it.

94

Keep tension out of your neck and shoulders. Look at the back of the ball and stroke through it to the hole, pulling the left hand along so that the left wrist goes through, guiding the blade. The right palm should stay square to the target line during the stroke. Stand still.

95

Let the arms and shoulders hang. The left hand grips under, with the wrist facing the target, or even a shade under the shaft. The hands should be ahead of the ball at address. Feature a very light grip, and minimize the action of the wrists during the stroke. Feel that your *shoulders are activating the stroke*.

96

To work out of a putting slump: Grip the club lightly to feel the head. The left pinky exerts a little pressure to keep out any wobble. Keep your head directly over the ball and fix your eyes on the exact spot where you intend to make contact. This will also prevent you from following the ball and mis-hitting it. When you drive a tack, you don't watch the hammer head!

97

The number one fundamental in putting: *Nothing should move but the arms. Keep still.*

Specialty Shots

98

Golf is a game of infinite variety played on landscapes of varying topography. You will confront new shots that require common sense and ingenuity. It's important that you understand the fundamentals for each shot.

99

Hitting the ball high: position the ball opposite your left heel and set up with *75 per cent of your weight back on your right foot*. This will automatically put your hands behind the ball and encourage a high trajectory regardless of the club you are using. During the downswing try not to transfer too much of your weight to your left side. Make a concerted effort to *hit with the right hand*, but ensure you do not turn it over through impact. This will give you a high trajectory, and will also promote accuracy. Use this same technique to get the ball up fast if you are blocked and have to get the ball up quickly over a tree.

100

Hitting the ball low: position the ball between the centre of your stance and your right foot. Grip the club firmly with both arms stretched. Comb or brush the grass going back for about 9 inches. Do the same after impact. Keep your weight on your left foot. This will restrict your backswing, thereby encouraging more of a punch shot.

101

Another method of hitting a low shot is to play the ball directly off your right heel, with about 70 per cent of your weight again on the left foot and remaining there. Break the wrists up abruptly and comb through the grass about 9 inches after impact. This should ensure that the left wrist does not cup. To encourage the low trajectory, keep the left arm and wrist very firm.

102

Intentional fade: Weaken your grip by *rolling your left wrist under the grip.* This will cause you to pick the club up more abruptly, thereby placing it outside the line. Because the right hand has effectively been

Fig. 16 Hitting the Ball High.
Your weight should favour your
right side, and the ball should be
opposite your left heel.

The right hand should be very
active in the hitting zone. This is
predominantly a wrist shot.

Focus your eyes under the back of
the ball.

Fig. 17   Hitting the Ball Low.
Position the ball between the centre
of your stance and your right foot.
Grip the club firmly with both arms
stretched.

Comb or brush the grass for 9
inches on the backstroke and also
after impact. This stroke is stiff-
armed, with no wrist action.

An alternate method that is also
effective is to play the ball opposite
your right heel, with your weight
70 per cent on your left foot. Break
your wrists up abruptly and comb
the grass for at least 9 inches after
impact. To prevent the left wrist
from cupping, keep your left arm
and wrist very firm.

Fig. 18   Intentional Slice.
Weaken the left grip so the Vs point
to your left shoulder. The right hand
should be placed in the normal
square position.

Place your feet in an open position,
with the left foot 6 to 8 inches back
from a square position and from
the line of the right foot.

This open position will promote a
swiping or cutting action at impact,
creating the desired left-to-right
spin of the ball. Aim the club face
at a target, well away from the
obstacle you are avoiding.

strengthened, and the club brought back outside, the clubface will be slightly open at impact. It will cut across the line to the target.

You will also encourage a fade by opening your stance at address. Do so by *pulling your left foot back from a square stance*. The ball will spin left to right, creating the fade. Be sure not to get fancy, however, and be certain to begin the flight of the ball well clear of the obstacle ahead of you. You will then get out of the trouble – your first objective – and the more the ball spins left to right, the closer you will get to your target. Point the clubface well left of your intended final target and clear of the trouble and the arcing shot will spin back into play.

103

Intentional hook: Assume a *closed stance by pulling your right foot back at least 6 inches* from a square stance. Play the ball more toward the right foot. Strengthen the grip by rolling the left wrist over to the right so that the V formed by the thumb and forefinger points to your right shoulder, and by placing the right hand more under the grip, with this V also pointing to your right shoulder. If your hands are in proper position for an intentional hook, you can see four knuckles on your left hand and only one on your right.

Be conscious of turning the right hip away from the ball on your backswing. The closed stance and strong grip will combine with this move to take the clubhead back inside a line drawn directly from the ball to the target and will produce a right-to-left spin on the ball. As always, when in trouble, pick a target wide enough of your obstacle to ensure that you will stay clear of it. Then the ball will hook according to the degree with which you have exaggerated the positions and moves above.

104

Uphill lie: Your right foot is lower than your left. This will create a higher trajectory, for which you will

Fig. 19 Intentional Hook.
First, set the Vs of both hands so
they point to your right shoulder.
Close the stance by pulling your
right foot at least 6 to 8 inches back
of and away from the line of your
left foot.

Pick a target well to the right of the
trouble you're avoiding to ensure a
successful shot. Aim the clubface
at your target.

need to compensate by taking steps to hit the ball the correct distance. Take a longer club to neutralize the effect of the higher ball flight, and place the ball opposite the middle of your stance. From this lie you are likely to hit a right-to-left shot, so allow for that by starting your ball more to the right of your target. Maintain an even rhythm.

105

Downhill lie: The bulk of your weight is on your left side. Play the ball more toward your right foot and select a club with a higher loft to compensate for the lower trajectory. Break up fast with your hands on the takeaway so that you will stay clear of the incline.

106

Sidehill lie, ball above your feet:
Your objective is to reduce the effect
of the abnormal conditions
imposed by the lie. Shorten your
grip on the club so that your
posture is somewhat more upright,
that is, more nearly normal. Open
your stance slightly to compensate
for the likelihood of a flat swing
and resulting hook. Maintain a firm
grip with the last three fingers of
your left hand so that your wrists
do not roll, and try to make the
back of your left hand proceed
through to the target. Take one club
extra because your swing will be
smaller due to the shorter grip and
restricted motion.

107

Sidehill lie, ball below your feet:
Lengthen your grip, or at least feel
it is lengthened, by holding the
club near its end. Because the ball
is lower than the soles of your feet,

you will need all the length of the club you can get. Position the ball in the middle of your stance and stand closer to the ball, even crowding it. This will keep you from turning your body on the backswing; since your power will be restricted, take one club extra. The ball will also fly left to right because of your tendency to swing towards your body from this lie. So aim more to the left of your target.

108

Fairway sand shots: Your first objective is to get out of the trap. *Select the club that will ensure you clear the lip of the trap.* Then worry about distance. For normal shots from fairway traps, play the ball back towards your right foot. This will help you hit down and through the ball. At address, place 70 per cent of your weight on your left heel, and keep most of it there during the swing. The ideal placement of the ball is just opposite the inside of your right heel. *You will*

swing the club in an upright arc.
The intent is to *hit the ball first* and
drive right through the sand with a
descending arc. Plant your feet
solidly for this shot.

109

Pick shots from traps cleanly,
without taking sand, from 50 yards
to green or more: Play off the right
foot and use a very upright
takeaway. Break the wrists up right
off the ball. Maintain a firm stance
in the sand to prevent slippage,
and hit the ball first, with the right
hand very active in the "hit zone."
Keep your focus on the back of the
ball. Anchor your right elbow lightly
on your right hip to maintain the
swing path. Use a 9 iron, pitching
wedge or sand iron depending on
the lip clearance.

Fig. 20 Long Fairway Bunker Shots.
Plant your feet firmly. Your weight should favour your left side. The ball should be opposite your right heel.

The backswing starts with an early break for a descending blow. Full follow-through is essential. The ball is struck first in the manner of a punch shot.

Problems and Cures / The Basics

110

Before you change anything in your swing, check the fundamentals. Be especially careful of your *alignment*. Ensure you are maintaining a *steady head position* from start to finish. Note the positions of your shoulders at address. Make certain they are square to your target. These are common errors that can easily creep into your game. Have a friend watch you, someone who knows your game.

Loss of control

111

This can occur when the back of your left wrist isn't flat at the top of your swing. Make sure you keep

your right elbow lightly in touch
with your side; your left wrist will
then be more likely to find the
correct position at the top.

Fast, flippy swing

112

If you are getting too quick, thereby
losing control of the clubhead and
tempo, you might be carrying your
hands too low at address. This
often causes a sloppiness in the
wrists. Raise the hands slightly.
Maintain grip pressure in the last
three fingers of your left hand,
thereby deadening the wrist. This
will also help keep your hands
together during the swing. Sole the
club lightly behind the ball and kiss
the grass gently to promote a
smooth, slow takeaway.

113

Fast and flippy often means a short backswing. This can wreck your timing and cause you to slap helplessly at the ball. A good way *to keep the backswing long and smooth* is to adopt in practice one of Moe Norman's ideas. Take a coin and lay it on the turf about 2 feet behind the ball. On your backswing, ensure you touch the coin with the sole of your club, thereby producing *a wide, low takeaway.* This drill also helps develop a one-piece backswing, where everything moves in unison, and a full shoulder turn.

114

Another way of guarding against too fast action is to take care not to grip the club too tightly with the right hand. Keep the pressure light, so that you can feel the clubhead. If the right hand pressure is tight, you are prone to jerking the club away from the ball.

Loss of power

115

Guard against allowing your hands to merely slide through the ball without any force. *Hit with your right hand* but do not overpower the pulling force of the left hand through impact.

116

A good way to gain more power is to concentrate on *turning your right shoulder* going back rather than your left shoulder. That gets the clubhead back easier, and also keeps the right elbow from flying away from your side. You need only insure that you don't take the club back too much on the inside. The move promotes a greater upper body turn, and hence more power. A *steady head is imperative*.

117 ▮▮▮▮▮▮▮▮▮▮▮▮

A common error that reduces power lies at the heart of the well-known and correct advice "swing, don't hit." The hit impulse is a chronic fault, particularly with the driver. Swing *through* the ball, not at it. Be aware also that it is so much easier to swing rather than hit if you keep your head still.

118 ▮▮▮▮▮▮▮▮▮▮▮▮

Power comes from *stability*. Think of a high jumper. He can't get any power if he is out of balance. Balance means keeping yourself swinging around an axis, a central point. Again, keep the head still, and you will find the necessary balance comes easier.

119 ▮▮▮▮▮▮▮▮▮▮▮▮

It's often helpful to turn your head slightly to the right a split second

before starting your backswing.
This gives your left shoulder room
to turn more fully under your chin,
and helps you focus on the back of
the ball.

Pushing the ball

120

A push, or a shot that starts to the
right and continues in that direction,
can result when you sway your
hips past the ball on the swing-
through. To avoid this, ensure that
your belt buckle goes to the target;
you will achieve this by *turning
through the ball*. *Rotate* your hips
going back and coming through.
Maintain your head position. Keep
your right heel in the bucket a little
longer.

121

You might also push the ball if you
allow your right knee and hip to
float forward. The right knee
should move towards the left knee

and both should move towards
the hole so that the inside of your
right thigh grazes your left thigh
through impact and the finish.

122

Pushing the ball can also result
when you put too much weight on
your left side at address. Get back
on your heels; put some weight on
your right side at address.

123

Another remedy for pushing is to
point your left knee at the ball at
address, and turn away from the
ball on your takeaway. Work your
right knee towards your left knee
on your downswing, not towards
the ball. This is also a superb
means of improving your alignment through the ball, as well as
going a long way towards
correcting a push shot.

Slicing

124

This most common error results when the clubface approaches the ball on an outside-in path. To avoid this, allow your right elbow to drive down and graze your right hip or side on the downswing. This will keep you on an inside path to the ball; indeed, you will find it impossible to get outside the line. Again, check that your right forearm is not higher than your left forearm at address. Also be sure that your shoulders and hips are not open.

Pulling

125

This occurs when a shot starts to the left and continues in that direction. One way to combat it is to raise your hands a shade at address. Also, check your shoulder and hip alignment, as well as your forearms so that the clubhead does not take an outside-to-in path wiping across the ball.

Hooking

126

A good way to keep from hooking is to clear your hips faster through the ball, and just let the clubhead pour through. If the hips stay back, the club tends to whip through on its own track, out of control, and invariably turns over, causing a hook. Additionally, your grip position could be too strong, with the Vs pointing too far right at address, causing your hands to roll in at impact. Also, check that your right foot is not pulled back into a closed stance and that your hands are not too low at address.

Reverse pivot

127

A reverse pivot occurs when you transfer your weight to the left side on your backswing and then to the right side on the downswing, falling away from the shot and losing power and control. To prevent this, set the club behind the ball at address using only your left hand when lining up the target. Do not move the shaft. This keeps you from leaning to the left at address, for after you have placed your right hand on the club, you have effectively put yourself in better balance. Lock or cock your right knee to the left at address. This will prevent your weight transfer from moving to the right side of your right shoe and the resulting loss of balance.

Swaying

128

You sway when you move too far off the ball on your takeaway. To avoid this, turn away from the ball with your right shoulder. Another way to think of the move is to sit back at address and feel 65 per cent of your weight on your right heel. *Turn your right pocket away from the ball* and get all your weight to the right heel on your backswing. Again, cock your right knee in, and rotate, like the point of a compass.

Fat shots

129

If you are scooping and hitting fat shots, as happens most frequently with a pitching wedge, weaken your left-hand grip and hit with your right hand. At address, keep your left arm taut, get in close, and keep your right elbow on your hip. Keep your head in the same place; don't dip.

130

You can also avoid fat shots by getting your hands forward while visualizing the path of the clubhead being directed *through* the hitting area for at least 14 inches. Let the hands flow *through to the hole*. Feel a sitting position at address, tummy sucked in, your back fairly straight and your head held steady.

Topping

131

This happens most often when you raise up through impact; it can also result from coming up anytime during the swing. Simply maintain your address posture through the swing. Remember: if you set up right, and imagine being in the same position at impact, you won't top the ball. *Stay down* and maintain your head position.

Final Reminders

I   Maintain a steady head position throughout the swing.
II   Keep your composure.
III   Your constant tempo and timing thought should be to swing your hands and arms at the same pace coming down as going up. This does not automatically happen; however, the thought of an identical pace up and down produces an idea tempo, a smooth rhythm, and your best timing.
IV   Feel relaxed in the neck area.

Selecting and Purchasing Your Golf Clubs

In today's economy, the purchase of a set of custom-built golf clubs represents a sizeable investment, so the purchaser should take his or her time to explore the features being offered by the multitude of manufacturers.

Most importantly, the selection of your equipment should be governed by your knowledge of the specifications that suit your type of game and swing. These would be the shaft flex, swing-weight, style of grip, size of grip, and shaft length.

Where individuals are very tall or short, or have long or short arms, consideration must be given to "longer" or "shorter" length shafts.

The correct advice can usually be obtained from your club professional. However, if you are not a member of a private club, you should seek out a professional whose expertise you respect.

Golf magazines such as *Golf* and *Golf Digest* carry ads and testimonials by many of the leading tour professionals who represent manufacturers. These ads unquestionably influence many buyers of golf equipment. However, I personally regard some of the claims of a "wider" or "larger sweetspot" or other claims with some scepticism. Through experience and a knowledge of engineering I consider many of these comments purely sales ploys that sound great to many prospective buyers. The centre of gravity or sweetspot can easily be identified by balancing a golf club head on the rubber end of a pencil and is undisputed as to its location. It is very important that you are aware of this point as it should be located in the lower centre portion of the blade.

The criteria which I personally follow after 50 years as a competitor is based on my past engineering and toolmaking professions. Firstly, I am very particular about the type and hardness of the steel used in the heads. I favour a soft stainless steel. This transmits a sensation to my hands at impact that is not sharp and has no ringing resonance with the ball coming off the blade at high velocity as is common with hard steel heads now in considerable evidence. Secondly, I look for a golf club whose face serrations or grooving take advantage of the regulations for width, depth, and spacing so that I can achieve maximum backspin.

Thirdly, I make an effort to find out if the manufacturer, when assembling the shaft into the head, has provided a metal-to-metal fit, which has much to do with the feel at impact. Finally, shafts that are manufactured today are very precise. It is vital that you have some idea as to the shaft flex that suits your swing when ordering or testing clubs. Shaft flexes range from regular to stiff to extra-stiff. One of these should suit your swing. For a charge one may have a manufacturer frequency-match your shafts in your set if you are fully aware of the frequency or flex point that suits you. (This is easily identified if you have a particular club in your old set that feels great, since it can be turned over to the manufacturer for testing.) For some time now, manufacturers have been prone to making their irons stronger or to adjust the lofts so that their customers feel that the brand they have purchased is more powerful because of extra yardage they are realizing versus their old set. I personally am not in favour of this move as standards for club manufacturers have been in existence for many years and I cannot resign myself that a number 7-iron should give you 165 yards of carry using a normal swing.

Finally, my policy and advice is *"try before you buy,"* as it's rare that a professional at a golf club will not be happy to let you test a set of clubs, either on the practice range or on the golf course, so that you have an opportunity to determine if the set you are contemplating best suits your swing and expectations.

A Final Word

Some years ago I recognized the value of taking films of the great golfers with whom I came in contact. I felt that if I had both a library of their thoughts and a visual record of their swings, then I could constantly reinforce my swing. And so over the years I amassed some 5,000 feet of film, taken at tournaments such as the Masters and Canadian Open. After watching these time and time again, I feel that the finest golfers have in common certain positions that form a unified and coordinated golf swing.

The dominant golfers are similar in these factors: posture at address, forearm position, takeaway from the ball, position of the wrists at the top, drive of the legs, position at impact, extension through the ball, and finish of the swing in balance. Above all else, they maintain a more or less steady head position that acts as a central axis for their swings.

Posture at Address

It is noticeable that today's golfers stand "tall" at the ball, their hands are not carried too low at address, the stomach is tucked in, the knees are slightly bent, and the chin is up and pointing slightly to the right. The seat appears as if they are sitting on a high stool. The right forearm is never in front of the left forearm and the shoulders are always square to the target.

Takeaway From the Ball

The extension from the shoulder to clubhead forms a single line. They have a low, smooth tempo to hip level and a full shoulder turn and hip turn to the top.

Position of Left Wrist at the Top

The back of the left wrist should be parallel with the left forearm at the top, never cupped. As a consequence, the right elbow points down, as required.

Drive of the Legs

As the downswing begins, a lateral shift to the left leg takes place with the right knee driving toward the target.

Position at Impact

The right shoulder is down, the left shoulder up, one line from clubhead to ball, the hips smoothly turned to target and the body bowed. The left wrist is square to the target. The clubface continues to stay square after impact.

Extension Through the Ball

The club now travels through the ball after impact with the right arm straightening and extending toward the target. The head stays down on the shot with the chin pointing behind the ball and resisting the golf club's momentum to swivel the head. At no time should the head rise up to look at the flight; rather, the head swivels and follows the flight, but only well after impact.

Finish the Swing in Balance

The fact that almost all top professionals on the tour finish their swings with the shaft ending up behind their back on full shots tells you one important thing. At no point during the follow-through do they decelerate. Practise this and you will finish the swing in balance.

Study these areas that the golfing greats have in common, examine the tips in this book and you will be on your way to becoming a consistently fine golfer.

Contributors to the Tips in This Book

Al Balding
Jerry Barber
Tommy Bolt
Julius Boros
Gay Brewer, Jr.
Gordon Brydson
Johnny Bulla
Jackie Burke, Jr.
Bob Charles
Bruce Crampton
Bobby Cruickshank
Jimmy Demaret
Roberto De Vicenzo
Dale Douglass
George Fazio
Jim Ferrier
Jack Fleck
Vic Ghezzi
Bob Gray, Jr.
Freddie Haas
Walter Hagen
Claude Harmon
Labron Harris
Dutch Harrison
Jay Hebert
Bill Kerr
Joe Kirkwood
Tom Kite
George Knudson
Ted Kroll

Ky Laffoon
Gene Lesch
Gene Littler
Bobby Locke
George Low
Bill Mawhinney
Jug McSpaden
Dick Metz
Kel Nagle
Byron Nelson
Bobby Nichols
Moe Norman
Ed (Porky) Oliver
Arnold Palmer
Gary Player
Smiley Quick
Henry Ransom
Lex Robson
Gene Sarazen
John Schlee
Horton Smith
Marlene Streit
Jimmy Thomson
Lee Trevino
Ellsworth Vines
Art Wall
Al Watrous
Bo Wininger
Craig Wood
Kermit Zarley

Nick Weslock was born in Winnipeg in 1917. Until his retirement in 1980, he was the president and co-owner of Wes-Park Automation Ltd., and is currently a product consultant and promotional sales representative with Accuform Golf Ltd. He is a Director of the Ontario Golf Association, and a member of the Essex, Glen Abbey and Brantford golf and country clubs and an honorary member of several other clubs.

Tournament Record

Canadian Amateur Champion	*four times*
Ontario Open Champion	*seven times*
Ontario Amateur Champion	*eight times*
Low Amateur, Canadian Open	*sixteen times*
Invited to the Masters	*four times*
Canadian Senior Champion	*six times*
Ontario Senior Champion	*eleven times*
Eisenhower World Cup Team Member	*five times*
Commonwealth Team Member	*five times*
Ontario Willingdon Cup Team	*twenty-five times*
Inducted Canada's Golf Hall of Fame	*1971*
Inducted Canada's Sports Hall of Fame	*1970*
RCGA Certified Handicap (Scratch)	*forty years*
OGA Certified Handicap (Scratch)	*forty years*

Index